ALASKA

A PICTURE MEMORY

Text
Bill Harris

Captions
Nicola Dent

Design
Teddy Hartshorn

Photography
Colour Library Books Ltd.

Commissioning Editor
Andrew Preston

Editor
David Gibbon

Production
Ruth Arthur
Sally Connolly
Neil Randles
Andrew Whitelaw

Director of Production
Gerald Hughes

ALASKA
A PICTURE MEMORY

CRESCENT BOOKS
NEW YORK · AVENEL, NEW JERSEY

Nobody in the United States gave much thought to Alaska from the time their government bought it from the Russians in 1867 until gold was discovered in the Klondike thirty years later, even though the biggest strikes were made across the border in the Yukon Territory of Canada.

Most American didn't know the difference anyway, but they did know that the best way to get at the gold was through Alaska. Of the thousands who went north, less than half were hardy enough to make the trip from Skagway across the Chilkoot Pass in the direction of Dawson. Many of them didn't even bother to make the attempt, but stayed in Alaska to try their luck there. The luckiest of the lot, as it turned out, found gold in spite of himself. He was a Swedish missionary working among the Eskimos on the Seward Peninsula, and his discovery would put the town of Nome on the map. But not before three of his fellow Swedes had it completely staked out with mining claims, mostly in their own names but with a few choice spots reserved for local military officials whose gratitude they knew would eventually come in handy. When the Americans began arriving they declared the claims illegal because of one of the very few U.S. laws that applied in Alaska at the time: it was forbidden for aliens to mark off mining claims. But the military men whose job it was to enforce the law chose to ignore the newcomers' demands. Open warfare between the would-be miners and their protectors was narrowly averted when more gold was discovered on a nearby beach. It was easier to get at than under the land the Swedes had locked up, and there seemed to be plenty to go around. In just a few weeks, two-thousand beachcombers picked up a million dollars worth of the stuff, and most of them didn't even have to invest in a pick and shovel. Before long thousands more were on the way, but none of them were as lucky as three Australians who, after a year of hard digging, came up with

$413,000 worth of gold. The next big strike, $1.5 million, was made by an American, but the best claims still belonged to the Swedes and the American prospectors resented it.

If there was no law to speak of in Nome at the turn of the century, there were lawyers, and three of them put their heads together to solve the problem and at the same time spread some of the wealth in their own direction. They went to Washington and organized the Alaska Gold Mining Company, with the influential political boss Alexander McKenzie as its president. The stock in the company was distributed, as McKenzie put it, "where it will do the most good," among influential senators and other key officials. Their plan was to pass a special law allowing the company to seize all mining claims made by aliens in Alaska, including any that had been sold by foreigners to American citizens. If the bill they introduced in Congress had passed, the Alaska Gold Mining Company would have taken control of all the gold on the Seward Peninsula. As it turned out, the proposed law was defeated after a month of heated debate, but McKenzie was not. He had another trick up his sleeve. He knew that President McKinley was about to appoint a judge to serve in the new district court at Nome, and McKenzie had enough influence to hand-pick the candidate.

In many ways, it was far better for the company to have a judge on its payroll than the law on its side. Whenever a mining claim came before the court, the judge had the power to place the mines in receivership until the case was settled. He also, of course, had the power to name the receivers, who felt duty-bound to give the gold from the disputed claims to the Alaska Gold Mining Company for safe keeping. The value of the gold in the company's accounts increased the value of its stock, and the rich got richer while the court dawdled over a mountain of cases.

Within a week of the new judge's arrival, the company

although the grant was only half as large as in other territories, it was better than nothing. In less than three years, some fifty laws were passed for the benefit of Alaska, giving them such things as the right to establish their own communities and to tax themselves to support them. Of the greatest significance, in 1912 the men in charge formally decreed that from that moment, "the Constitution shall have the same force and effect within Alaska as elsewhere in the United States." The irony was lost on them that the treaty that brought it under U.S. control forty-five years earlier had quite specifically guaranteed Alaskans, "all the rights, advantages and immunities of citizens of the United States." The promise had been extended to everyone, including the Russians among them, though not the "uncivilized native tribes."

If the early days of Alaska's history were a disaster, they went a long way toward molding the character of today's Alaskans. Their official name for the state is "The Last Frontier" and the frontier spirit infects people quickly once they move there. Whether they are oilfield workers transplanted from the Southwest or escapees from the crowded Northeast, once they move up to America's Northwest corner their outlook changes even more than their lifestyle. Their newspapers concentrate more on local issues than national and international affairs, and when news creeps in from one of the other forty-nine states, it is usually characterized as word from "Outside." And after so many years of being treated as outsiders in the American family, it seems entirely appropriate.

But what makes the story of Alaska's neglect so bizarre is that it takes some doing to ignore it. If its 57,000-square-mile bulk were divided in half, both halves would be bigger than Texas, and there would be enough territory left over to squeeze in the State of Indiana. A trip that cuts across four international time zones from east to west within Alaska's borders is 2,400 miles, about the same as the distance between New York and Los Angeles. From north to south, the trip is close to 1,400 miles, about what a flier logs on a flight from Chicago to Phoenix. Alaska's seacoast, measuring about 44,000 miles on two oceans and three seas, is fifty percent longer than the shoreline of the combined lower forty-eight states. Minnesota claims to have ten thousand lakes, but Alaska has three million of them. It has a dozen major river systems, too, and 119 million acres of forest, as well as the highest mountains in North America. Mt. McKinley is the highest of them all, but of the top thirty on the continent, seventeen are in Alaska. It has forty-seven active volcanoes and five-thousand glaciers forever rearranging parts of the landscape.

Still, the landscape of Alaska seems solid and enduring, and though conservationists get apoplectic about such things as oil pipelines and super tankers and roads cut through the tundra, it is no less a pristine wilderness than any of the fifty states. Which is probably why official Washington still refuses to classify any of it except Anchorage as anything but rural. Even the capital city of Juneau is lumped into the statistical no-man's land most Americans equate with the wheatfields of Kansas. Considering the numbers, the government statisticians might be right. There is less than one Alaskan for every square mile of territory, but more than sixty-three percent of them live in cities. In Anchorage, for instance, the density shoots up to one hundred per square mile. But, of course, according to the people who classify such things, that's why it is the only official city in the state.

But do Alaskans care? Not on your life. They've been misunderstood from Day One, and they've long-since gotten used to it. And the last thing anyone on the New Frontier ever wants to be called is a city slicker, anyway.

Facing page: common to many parts of Alaska, the caribou differs from other deer in that both sexes have antlers, with those of the mature bull sometimes reaching four feet from base to tip. Traveling in large herds, caribou are constantly on the move, migrating from calving to wintering grounds, and feeding by light browsing that is perfectly suited to the slow-growing plants of the Alaskan tundra.

Originally known as Harrisburg, Alaska's capital, Juneau (these pages), was founded by two gold prospectors, Dick Harris and Joe Juneau, in the early 1900s. With its shingled and weatherboarded houses, and a population of around 30,000, Juneau still has a small-town atmosphere, despite its frenetic gold-rush origins. Top left: the Tourist Information Center, a re-creation of the town's first nineteenth-century log church, which later became a brewery. Facing page top: the ornate Governor's Mansion, completed in 1913 after Juneau replaced Sitka as territorial capital in 1906.

Below and center right: spectacular views of fjords and glaciers and the grandeur of the coastal mountains reward passengers of the frequent cruise ships that are attracted to the Alaskan coastline. Bottom right: floatplanes near Juneau, a common sight in Alaska, offer fascinating excursions to the surrounding area. Top right: skiing is a major winter sport in Alaska; pictured here are the chairlifts leading to the slopes of Eagle Nest ski resort, near Juneau. Overleaf: pleasure craft on Auke Bay.

A major tourist attraction, several of Juneau's impressive glaciers can be reached by road or viewed from the air. Below, top left and overleaf: the best known of Juneau's great rivers of ice is the Mendenhall Glacier, 13 miles north of the town. Meandering downwards for about 12 miles, the glacier originates from the 1,500-square-mile Juneau Ice Field. Center and bottom left: Glacier Bay National Park attracts nature lovers, wildlife watchers and fishermen.

On the southeast coast and about 90 miles northwest of Juneau, Glacier Bay National Park and Preserve encompasses about 3.3 million acres. Sixteen massive glaciers flow into the bay, including the blue-tinted Adams Inlet Glacier (right). With its diverse physical environment, Glacier Bay supports a wide range of wildlife, which includes extensive seal colonies (facing page bottom), the brown bear (bottom right), whales, sea lions, otters, mountain goats and a great variety of birdlife (top right).

Below: a spectacular aerial view of the Alaska Range with Mount Kimball in the distance. Left: the majestic volcanic cone of Mount Drum, in the Wrangell Mountains, overlooks the airport at Gulkana. This can be viewed by travelers on the Richardson Highway from Valdez to Delta Junction, along with Mount Sanford and Mount Wrangell. Center left: a small Alaskan boat harbor encircled by snow-covered mountains. Bottom left: a picturesque winter scene near Valdez. Overleaf: an impressive sunset at Mineral Creek, Valdez.

Right: large information boards provide visitors with facts about the famous Alaska oil pipeline and the range of wildlife in this area. Below: an aerial view of the trans-Alaska pipeline, which extends 800 miles from the northern Prudhoe Bay field, southward to the Valdez terminal on Prince William Sound, generally following the Richardson Highway. Overleaf: a raised section of the pipeline that passes near the city of Fairbanks. Oil development has led to a large influx of both people and money to Fairbanks.

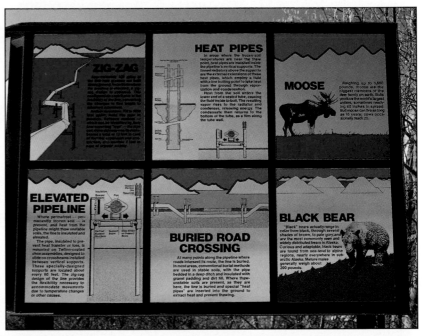

Often considered a frozen and desolate wasteland, the Delta River region of the Alaska Range (these pages) is a good example of the breathtaking scenery that can be found in Alaska. Left: one of many wooded lakes in the Delta Junction region that attract numerous fishermen and wildlife watchers. Center left: a raised section of the 800-mile-long, trans-Alaska oil pipeline. Bottom left: the spectacular Black Rapids, Delta River region.

Fairbanks (facing page), like many Alaskan cities, owes its origins to the arrival of gold prospectors in the early 1900s. Above and below: panning for gold. Situated on the bank of the River Chena, the area around Fairbanks is still a popular place for gold digging, although its main importance today is as a supply center for the interior. Left: a roadside restaurant. Center left: the stern-wheeler, Discovery II, *on the Tanana River, near Fairbanks. Bottom left: a disused gold dredge – reminder of the past dominance of gold prospecting in this region.*

The Richardson Highway, Alaska's first road, extends 368 miles from Valdez to Fairbanks via Delta Junction. This is a varied and beautiful scenic route through the magnificent Chugach Mountains and Alaska Range, leading past spectacular glaciers, gorges and rivers, through dense, green spruce forests (facing page) and across tundra meadows. Below: the broad Mat-Su Valley, Alaska's "breadbasket," and one of two major agricultural areas in the state. Fertile soil and long daylight hours result in giant specimens of many vegetables, including cabbages weighing up to 60lb.

Denali National Park (these pages), one of the world's greatest wildlife sanctuaries, surrounds awe-inspiring Mount McKinley. This area not only possesses dramatic views of gorges, rivers, forests and snow-covered mountains, but is also home to many wild animals – the grizzly bear (above), caribou (below), moose, Dall sheep, wolf and lynx, among others. With the completion of the Anchorage to Fairbanks Highway, the number of visitors has risen to more than 14,000 each year.

37

Below: Mount McKinley, at 20,320 feet, is the highest and most spectacular mountain in North America. Known by Alaskan Indians as Denali, or "the Great One," this peak dominates the 600-mile-long Alaska Range. Facing page: the formidable Ruth Glacier inches its way down the Mount McKinley massif. Overleaf: the Susitna River, overlooked by towering Denali.

Below and bottom right: Lake Hood, near Anchorage, claims to be the world's largest floatplane airport. The planes are equipped with floats for water landings and this eases the problem of finding suitable landing sites in the rugged landscape. Charter services operating from this, and other lakes, offer an excellent way to see the surrounding countryside. Top right: Anchorage International Airport, and (center right) the airport's helicopter base. Overleaf: an aerial view of Anchorage.

The town of Portage, surrounded by spectacular scenery (facing page bottom), lies some 50 miles southeast of Anchorage. Top right: Portage Creek, which carries silt-laden glacial meltwater from Portage Glacier and Portage Lake to Turnagain Arm. Above, left and below: Turnagain Arm, the thin finger of Cook Inlet near Portage, attracts numerous fishermen to its waters. Bottom left: a typical panoramic view from the Seward Highway. Overleaf: Explorer Glacier, one of eight in the Portage Glacier Recreational Area.

Bottom left: Portage Creek, Kenai Fjords National Park. Left: Aialik Bay, at the tip of the Harding Icefield (center left), is dramatic with its stark surrounding peaks and still waters, colored a deep blue by the sky. Below: glacier in Aialik Bay, near Seward, one of over thirty-four glaciers originating from the massive Harding Icefield, a remnant of the Ice Age that caps a section of the Kenai Mountains. Overleaf: tide-water glaciers, perhaps the most impressive of these huge rivers of ice.

Right and facing page top: with the majestic Kenai Mountains behind, the fishing town of Homer sits on the shore of Kachemak Bay, famous for its variety of marine life. Above and facing page bottom: boat marina at Seward. Once Alaska's leading port city, Seward has regained its prosperity after the 1964 earthquake devastated its economy. Top right: the Russian church and cemetery at Ninilchik, a reminder that Alaska was once part of the Russian empire. Bottom right: vividly painted Indian "spirit houses" and the Russian Orthodox church (below) at Eklutna, near Anchorage.

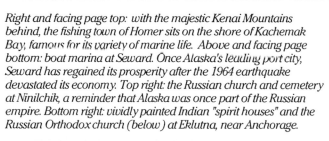

The challenging Iditarod Trail Sled Dog Race (above and below), a world-famous, 1,049-mile marathon from Anchorage to Nome (overleaf), crosses two mountain ranges – the Alaska and the Kuskokwim – passes along the wide Yukon River, through tiny villages, such as Nikolai (left) and across empty miles of tundra. Top left: airplanes on Iditarod Lake. Facing page bottom: sunset at Amalakleet. Facing page top: satellite station on the Bering Sea, Nome, some 30 miles south of the Arctic Circle. Final page: frozen Norton Sound, on the Bering Sea.